By Elizabeth Dennis   Illustrated by Natalie Kwee

Ready-to-Read

SIMON SPOTLIGHT

An imprint of Simon & Schuster Children's Publishing Division
1230 Avenue of the Americas, New York, New York 10020
This Simon Spotlight edition December 2019
Text copyright © 2019 by Simon & Schuster, Inc.
Illustrations copyright © 2019 by Natalie Kwee
Manufactured in the United States of America 1019 LAK
2 4 6 8 10 9 7 5 3 1
Library of Congress Cataloging-in-Publication Data
Names: Dennis, Elizabeth, author. ǀ Kwee, Natalie, illustrator.
Title: If you love cooking, you could be ... / by Elizabeth Dennis ; illustrated by Natalie Kwee.
Description: Simon Spotlight edition. ǀ New York : Simon Spotlight, 2019. ǀ Series: Ready-to-reads ǀ Summary: "A
nonfiction Level 2 Ready-to-Read about careers in the food and cooking industry: chef, cook, recipe developer, and food
stylist"—Provided by publisher. Identifiers: LCCN 2019029442 (print) ǀ LCCN 2019029443 (ebook) ǀ ISBN 9781534454545
(hardcover) ǀ ISBN 9781534454552 (trade paperback) ǀ ISBN 9781534454569 (ebook) Subjects: LCSH: Cooking—Vocational
guidance—Juvenile literature. ǀ Food industry and trade—Vocational guidance—Juvenile literature.
Classification: LCC TX652.4 .D46 2019 (print) ǀ LCC TX652.4 (ebook) ǀ DDC 641.5023—dc23 • LC record available at
https://lccn.loc.gov/2019029442 • LC ebook record available at https://lccn.loc.gov/2019029443

Glossary

Chef: one of the leaders of a professional kitchen who helps decide the menu and manages the other people in the kitchen

Cook: a person who makes food in a restaurant or another place that serves food

Dish: food that is cooked and prepared as part of a meal

Food stylist: a person who arranges food for photos and videos used in cookbooks, commercials, and more

Ingredient: a food item that is included in a recipe

Recipe: a list of ingredients and instructions for how to prepare a dish

Recipe developer: a person who creates new recipes for food magazines, cookbooks, and restaurants

Note to readers: Some of these words may have more than one definition. The definitions above are how these words are used in this book.

Contents

Introduction   4

Chapter 1: Cook and Chef   6

Chapter 2: Recipe Developer   14

Chapter 3: Food Stylist   22

More Cool Food Jobs!   32

WARNING: This is not a cookbook. If you would like to cook, never use the kitchen without adult supervision.

Introduction

Do you love cooking and baking?
Do you like watching cooking shows
and trying new foods?

Did you know that some people cook every day as part of their jobs? When you grow up, you could work with food too!

Chapter 1:
Cook and Chef

If you love making food,
you could be a cook
or a chef.

Many cooks and chefs
work in restaurants and hotels.
Some cooks work in school cafeterias,
making food for students like you.
Others work in people's homes
and are called private chefs.

In a restaurant, each cook works at a different cooking station. They might be in charge of grilling, frying, or using the stove.

A chef is a cook and a leader.
They are in charge of other people
in the kitchen and help create
the restaurant's menu.

Cooks and chefs have to be strong.
They lift heavy pots and pans
and spend many hours on their feet.
They also work long hours,
at night, and on the weekends.
That is when many people
go out to eat!

Teamwork is also important.
Many people work together
to prepare the food quickly.
When everyone is moving
in different directions, the kitchen
can look like a dance studio!

Some cooks go on to become
assistant chefs or chefs.
No matter what their job is,
they all love food.

If you want to grow up
to be a cook or chef,
you can practice cooking
with a grown-up. You can even
take a cooking class!

Chapter 2:
Recipe Developer

If you enjoy mixing foods and flavors,
you could develop recipes
(say: RESS-i-peez).
A recipe is a set of step-by-step
instructions to make a dish,
like macaroni and cheese.

A recipe also includes a list of foods
called ingredients
(say: in-GREE-dee-ehnts)
and the amounts that are needed.
A macaroni and cheese recipe
might include one pound of pasta
as an ingredient.

Recipe developers come up with recipes for cookbooks, magazines, and websites. Some work with chefs to create recipes for restaurant menus.

Being a recipe developer is
like being a scientist.
Each recipe begins with an idea.
Then the recipe developer
experiments with ingredients,
cooking times, and temperatures.
It might take fifteen or more tries
before the dish tastes just right!

Just like a scientist,
recipe developers always take notes.
This way, they know how to make
the exact same dish again.

They also use a lot of math.
For example, if they use
three wedges of cheese
and just a bit of milk,
the cheese sauce
might become lumpy.
If they use one wedge of cheese
and a lot of milk,
it might become runny.

Recipe developers are experts
on taste and texture.
They know that if they roast
a vegetable until it turns brown,
it becomes sweet and crispy.
The high heat turns
the vegetable's natural sugars
into a kind of caramel.

If you want to be a recipe developer, try experimenting with flavors. What happens if you add cinnamon to cereal or salt to berries? The combinations are endless!

Chapter 3: Food Stylist

Have you ever seen a photo or video
of food that looked so tasty,
it made you hungry?
That was thanks to a food stylist!
Food stylists make food look good
in cookbooks, advertisements,
websites, and more.

Food stylists start with the recipe
of the dish they will style,
like a cheeseburger.
They use it to make a shopping list.

Then they go to the store
to pick out the freshest ingredients.
They might look through hundreds
of tomatoes to find the roundest,
reddest, and smoothest ones.

Before stylists start cooking the dish,
they choose plates and other details
with the photographer
and other staff.
Then it is time to cook!

Stylists work quickly
to arrange the food
before the cheese hardens,
the bread gets soggy,
or the lettuce wilts.

They use tweezers to arrange
small things so they look just right.
Sometimes they brush oil
on the food to make it shiny.

In the past, food stylists
used unsafe things like glue
to make food look perfect.
Now they make food look real
with crumbs and drips,
and the food can actually
be eaten after it's styled!

If you want to be a food stylist, you can practice arranging your own food so it looks fresh and tasty.

If you love food and cooking, you can read cookbooks and food magazines. You can also help make food at home.

Someday you might invent recipes and cook beautiful meals for your friends, family, and many more people!

Chef, cook, recipe developer, and food stylist are just a few cool jobs for people who love food. Turn the page to discover even more!

More Cool Food Jobs!

A **farmer** grows fruit, vegetables, grains, and other food for people to eat. Sometimes they raise animals like chickens and cows.

A **food critic** (say: KRIT-tick) writes their opinions about restaurants and other food services. They usually work for newspapers, magazines, or websites.

A **food photographer** takes photographs of food that are used for magazines, cookbooks, advertisements, and websites.

A **nutritionist** (say: new-TRISH-un-ist) helps people choose what to eat so they can be healthy.

A **pastry chef** is a cook who is an expert at making desserts and baked foods like cookies, cakes, and pies.

A **restaurant manager** takes care of the money and the business tasks for a restaurant. They order supplies, hire new workers, and keep track of workers' schedules.